SELF-IMAGE

JAMES "TRIP" MOORE

Dr. Tom Varney
Series Editor

NAVPRESS

BRINGING TRUTH TO LIFE
NavPress Publishing Group
P.O. Box 35001, Colorado Springs, Colorado 80935

The Navigators is an international Christian
organization. Jesus Christ gave His followers
the Great Commission to go and make
disciples (Matthew 28:19). The aim of The
Navigators is to help fulfill that commission by multiplying laborers for Christ in
every nation.

NavPress is the publishing ministry of The
Navigators. NavPress publications are tools
to help Christians grow. Although publications alone cannot make disciples or change
lives, they can help believers learn biblical
discipleship, and apply what they learn to
their lives and ministries.

© 1992 by James Moore
All rights reserved. No part of this pub-
     lication may be reproduced in any
     form without written permission from
     NavPress, P.O. Box 35001, Colorado
     Springs, CO 80935.
ISBN 08910-96841

Third printing, 1993

Cover illustration: David Watts

The anecdotal illustrations in this book
are composites of real situations, and any
resemblance to people living or dead is
coincidental.

Printed in the United States of America

CONTENTS

❧

FOREWORD

ৈ

As we near the end of the twentieth century, the church is facing two monstrous dangers. One is the ongoing and strengthened tendency to treat people like dogs who can be trained to obey without offering more than the tokens of relationship.

The truth of *biblical sufficiency* (a position that teaches that the answers to all of life's non-physical problems can be found in Scripture) has been corrupted into an ugly perversion that permits us to use the Bible as a bludgeon to coerce conformity. Sin is often defined as nothing more than clear transgressions of understood rules. "Biblical" counseling, in some circles, has become a matter of looking for patterns of behavioral irresponsibility, finding passages that condemn those patterns and command better ones, and then requiring people to do what they should under threat of judgment.

Directing hurting people to the Word of God and to prayer and to Christ, when done this way, actually leads people away from the message of God's Word (that we are people who, because of His mercy, can enjoy a relationship with Him that will prompt obedience). This method robs prayer of its relational dimension and makes it more like filling out a form for a bureaucrat with a request for aid. It makes Christ into more a Gestapo commander than a bridegroom.

This trend, stubbornly present in so many fundamentalist circles, is awful. But there is an opposite trend, equally bad, that begins well.

Sweeping through our entire culture is the idea that people matter more than rules, that opportunities for fulfillment and self-esteem are more important to emphasize than our responsibilities to do what we should. This second trend, the cult of self-esteem, recognizes that we are not dogs who can be trained but rather people who long to be in relationship. And that's good.

But this good beginning has turned sharply in a wrong direction. We have become consumed with feeling good about ourselves. Finding release from shame has taken priority over doing good for someone else; recovering a sense of our own value has become more important than seeing to it that our lives reflect favorably on Christ.

Within Christian circles, the preoccupation with developing a good self-image has changed the way we think about God. He has now become a useful source of self-esteem. His function is to boost our appreciation for ourselves. When He comes through, we feel good toward Him—and we call those good feelings worship.

I'm not sure which trend disturbs me more. The first requires us to deaden our souls, to kill all passion except anger and discipline. We become shallow, rigid people who remain, at best, warmly courteous but incapable of intimacy. The second encourages us to release our passions, but in the wrong direction. We become not dead, but alive like a cancer growing out of control. We become the point of life. Our glory (defined as the recognition of our value) becomes the thing to reclaim. God's glory is reduced to helping us with that project.

The first trend makes too little of our hurt. The second one makes too much of it. God cares that we hurt. He never intended that we live with the sort of self-hatred that seems to reliably develop in the presence of uncaring parents and friends.

But He also maintains that His glory is more important for us to concern ourselves with than our hurt. And when we get it right, we discover that it is God's glory to replace our hurt with joy.

Trip Moore tackles the topic of self-image with a felt concern for the pain of self-hatred. His is no dog-theology that teaches us to fetch for the master to avoid the stick and win a biscuit. He is also concerned to steer us away from a preoccupying pursuit of a better self-image. Only in pursuit of Christ does our longing to find value in our unique existence fall clearly into place. Trip Moore knows that!

If you read his thinking rightly, you'll not bother with recovering your self-esteem. Nor will you treat how badly you sometimes feel about yourself as a minor problem to be buried beneath an avalanche of disciplined good works. Rather, you will come to understand that a unique passion can be restored within you, a passion that will free you not to love yourself more but to contribute to the eternal purposes of God.

God has given us something far more interesting to think about than ourselves. As we enter into the mystery of life as revealed in Christ and lose ourselves in all that He is up to, we one day realize we've found ourselves as well—and we devote all that we find to strengthening His reputation, not to building our self-image. Because then there is no need to.

DR. LARRY CRABB

7

INTRODUCTION

THE BATTLE WITH A POOR SELF-IMAGE

It happened to me again this morning. I had just shut off the alarm clock and was lying there thinking about facing my day. All of a sudden, I became aware of a strong sense of not liking the "me" I was about to remove from the bed and move into my world.

There it was again: an all-too-familiar (and yet never friendly) voice that regularly stops me in my tracks and brings my whole life and purpose into question. A voice that so convincingly portrays me as small, inadequate, undesirable, insignificant . . . I could compose quite a formidable list of accusatory words. Why do I hate myself so much sometimes?

One thing that intrigues me most about these bouts with my negative image is the times when they seem to occur. How can a guy dislike himself so much at the beginning of his day, when he hasn't even had time to do anything wrong yet? Why do such thoughts sometimes seem strongest when I'm just about to taste success as a result of having done something really well? A couple of years ago, I gave a very successful weekend conference that people obviously enjoyed and benefited from. The intriguing question is, why did I find myself, right afterward, feeling like a failure and a fraud? It's almost as if I won't allow myself to be good. Why would I hold on to seeing myself as bad?

I am aware of the dynamics of "self-image." I've thought long and hard, even given lectures, on the cause of a bad self-image. I'm writing this discussion guide! Yet, in spite of all my knowledge, I remain prone to that often overwhelmingly strong feeling of not being what I really need to be in order to make it in my world. What's happening here?

This struggle with a negative view of ourselves is a key part of the overall spiritual battle we face. And if my experience is normative, a bad self-image isn't transformed by a theoretical knowledge of what's going on.

What, then, is required to allow us to taste freedom from these thoughts and feelings that often paralyze us and keep us from living in ways that glorify God? This discussion guide will help answer that question.

GROWING TOGETHER

In those moments when the way I see myself makes all seem hopeless, part of the consolation I feel is in knowing I'm not alone in such struggles. While not many of us share openly with others these feelings that get so close to how we really see ourselves, I have the privilege as a counselor of spending many hours each week talking with men and women about what is happening in their lives. It seems *everyone* struggles, to some degree, with a negative self-image.

Somehow just knowing that is a key part of being able to deal effectively and biblically with our poor self-image. To know people who battle with a strong, negative self-image and yet succeed in touching others on God's behalf somehow robs me of some of the "disqualifying effects" of my own negative self-image. On many occasions when I've been overwhelmed by feelings of inadequacy and have felt like giving up, I've been reminded of something a dear friend once shared with me. He said he often feels like an insignificant,

unqualified little boy who wants to flee before chal-
lenges and opportunities. It motivates me to know that
he, too, faces such struggles, and yet to watch him move
into his world in ways that are changing people's lives
(like writing the foreword in this guide). I am inspired
to discover the freedom that the Lord offers me to be
able to live in the same way.

We were never meant to struggle in a vacuum.
Growth is a community affair. Just learning that my
friend struggles with the same tendencies I do encourages me to face my battles and not give up. Some of
us simply pretend all is well in an effort to hide the
true selves we find so hideous. If we do this, we not
only end up alone in the battle, but our struggles never
become an influence to encourage others' perseverance
and growth.

I hope this guide will become an opportunity for
many to discover and share together some of our inner
workings — "the thoughts and attitudes of the heart"
(Hebrews 4:12) — not as an end in itself, but in an effort
to expose those realities that can drive us passionately
to the One who offers us "mercy and . . . grace to help
us in our time of need" (verse 16).

USING THIS GUIDE

This guide can be used in any one of three ways: (1) on
your own; (2) with a group after prior preparation at
home; or (3) with a group with no prior preparation.

It's amazing how another person's story can spark
insights into our own situation. A discussion group
shouldn't get larger than twelve people, and four to
eight is ideal. If your group is larger than eight, one
way to be sure everyone gets plenty of time to talk is to
divide into subgroups of four to discuss. This approach
can accommodate even a large Sunday school class.

You'll get the most out of the guide if you use both
prior preparation and group discussion. Group members can read the text of a session and reflect on the
questions during the week. They might keep a journal

handy to jot down thoughts, feelings, and questions to bring to the group time. This approach allows time for participants to recall and reflect upon incidents in their lives.

However, a group can also approach the sessions "cold" by reading the text aloud and answering the questions together. If busy schedules make homework impractical, feel free to take this approach.

Finally, if you're using this guide on your own, you'll probably want to record your responses in a journal.

The guide is designed to be covered in five sessions of sixty to ninety minutes each. However, you could spend a lot more time on some questions. If you have plenty of time, you may want to travel through the guide at your group's own speed.

Each session contains the following sections:

A warm-up question. You'll be coming to sessions with your mind full of the events of the day. To help you start thinking about the topic at hand, the sessions begin with a warm-up question. It sometimes refers to what you've observed about yourself during the previous week. At other times, it invites participants to let the others get to know them better.

Text. You'll find words of insight into the topic in each session. Sometimes the text appears all in one chunk; at other times questions fall between blocks of text. You'll probably want someone (or several people) to read the text aloud while the others follow along. Alternatively, you could take a few minutes for each participant to read it silently. If you've all read the text at home, you can skip reading it again.

Discussion questions. These will help you understand what you've read and consider how it relates to your own experience and struggles. Each participant's stories will shed light on what the others are going through.

When the text is broken into two or more sections, with questions in between, you should discuss the questions before going to the next section of text.

Many questions ask participants to talk about themselves. Everyone should feel free to answer at his or her own level of comfort. People will often feel some discomfort if a group is really dealing honestly with issues. However, participants should not feel pressured to talk more personally than they wish. As you get to know each other better, you'll be able to talk more freely.

Prayer. Ideas for closing prayer are offered as suggestions. You may already have a format for praying in your group, or you may prefer not to pray as a group. Feel free to ignore or adapt these ideas.

During the week. In this section you'll find ideas for trying what you've learned and for observing your daily behavior more closely. Feel free to do something else that seems more helpful.

Process notes. The boxed instructions will help the leader keep the group running smoothly. There are also leader's notes at the end of this guide.

FOR MORE BACKGROUND

Whether you're a group leader or a participant, or using this guide on your own, you'll find it helpful to read the introduction to this series from the Institute of Biblical Counseling (IBC): *Who We Are and How We Relate* by Dr. Larry Crabb. It explains the approach to personal growth taught at IBC—the reasoning behind this series' approach to handling problems.

FLEEING FROM ANGUISH:
How a Self-Image Develops

ह

1. Which of these do you think best describes you right now?

   ❑ I think of myself more highly than I should.

   ❑ I think less of myself than I should.

   ❑ Both (explain).

   ❑ Neither (explain).

LEADER: To begin, let each participant answer question 1. If you don't already know each other, introduce yourselves as you answer the question.

Ask someone (or several people) to read the following text aloud. As the participants listen and read along, they should underline or star statements they identify with.

A RAW NERVE

When I was about ten years old, my mother gave me a Ken doll for Christmas so I could play with my younger sisters and their Barbies. That, in itself, is a disturbing memory. But the part I remember most vividly was when my father came into the room and argued with my mother over giving me a doll. There I was, sitting on the living room floor playing dolls with my sisters, listening to my parents argue. Suddenly, my father looked at me with disgust and walked out of the room. I don't recall that any more was ever said about the Ken doll. I only know that those few minutes marked me indelibly with a sense of being a little guy who was somehow fundamentally defective. My father's expression had said it all.

The subject of self-image has amazing potential to shake us to the core. When I shared my story among friends recently, I got back in touch with some scary feelings and troubling questions: "What is wrong with me that my own dad finds me disgusting?" "Am I a normal male, or is something basically not right?" At the same time, I saw again how good I am at living in ways that keep me from having to face such feelings and questions very often—although I know they lie just beneath the surface and influence me daily.

As uncomfortable as such reflections are, I'm convinced we need to embrace them if we wish to get beyond simply being victims of our bad self-images. Our consideration of self-image will move us toward freedom only to the degree that we allow it to touch us at a level that stirs up our uncomfortable memories and questions. As you work through this material, try to be open to facing stories from your past that provide the emotional fuel for the self-image that controls you.

A QUESTION EVERY CHILD ASKS

Why do disturbing childhood events carry such power to shake me even thirty years later? What's going on inside a child that lets a disdainful look or an angry word have such impact?

The answer begins at creation, when God made us

in His image. He designed us to be relational beings like Him, capable of touching others in deep ways and of being touched by them. As a result, every child arrives in the world with a deep thirst for relationship. The infant carries an inborn longing for something he simply *has* to find in order to survive as a person—something he cannot find within himself.

What is every child looking for? A relationship with someone who accepts and takes pleasure in her *just as she is*; a relationship in which she is regarded as someone with something of value to offer her world. Every child arrives asking, "Is there anyone in my world who loves and values me for who I am?" Or, put another way, "Am I a lovable and valuable person?" Such questions are rarely asked consciously. They nevertheless put us in contact with the uncomfortable fact that we are fundamentally dependent (I *need* someone outside myself) and, therefore, very vulnerable.

A child turns toward the most important people in his world to find the kind of relationship his heart was made to need desperately. Then he makes a deeply disturbing discovery: He simply is *not* loved as much as he needs to be, and he is *not* as important to his parents (friends, etc.) as he longs to be.

All of us have faced this fact in painful ways. Some of us were simply ignored or treated with indifference. Others were given a place of importance and pampered, but in ways that seemed to miss who we really were and made us feel indebted. Others were taken advantage of and used, some even sexually. Others were ridiculed.

One woman I know was dressed in rags while her little sister was given fancy dresses. Another friend of mine pleaded for months for a bike of his own. When his parents finally gave in to his request, it was with looks of contempt and the message, "You're a selfish little boy."

2. a. Take a minute to think of one of your "Ken doll" stories (a time when someone important let you

17

know you were a disappointment). Jot a note if it helps you bring the scene back.

b. Because those incidents come wrapped in shame, it's often hard to talk about them, even with people you know well. Each of you should have an opportunity to tell either (1) your story and the message it sent, or (2) just the message you heard from the disapproving person(s). Don't feel pressured to tell your story, even if everyone else in the group does.

c. What feelings do you have as you share these events and their effects? (Do you find yourself withdrawing, getting tears in your eyes, feeling pain in your chest or stomach? Do you find your-self feeling nothing at all?)

3. How aware are you today of longing to be deeply enjoyed and valued?

❑ Intensely aware

❑ A little aware

❑ Not aware at all

Your level of awareness:

LEADER: Read this section aloud. Each participant should consider whether he or she has deadened his or her longing heart.

OUR SCRAMBLE TO SURVIVE

What happens when we admit we don't matter to our world the way we deeply need to matter? First of all, we experience extreme pain, the deepest ache of human existence. It is the pain of feeling unlovable and without value (a sample of hell), multiplied by the fact that we are unable to find that which we simply *must* have to survive. As a result, there is a panic attached to the pain, much like we would feel upon discovering we were trapped in our car in a snowbank with no food or water and little hope of being rescued.

A second result is seen in what we do not do when we face this crisis. In our desperate need, *we do not seek God* — at least not in the ultimate sense of what that should mean. Because we are descended from Adam and Eve, our natural preference is to come up with a solution to our problem *on our own*. But God designed us with longings for love that He knew only He could satisfy. In spite of this, we refuse to turn to the only One in the universe who truly loves us for who we are and thrills over our potential value. Because of this refusal we are left to ourselves to find a solution to the fact that our world doesn't provide us with what we demand that it provide.

From that point on, our rebellious independence takes us in some harmful directions. The first step we take to relieve our pain is to try to deaden our longing heart. It's as if the child says to himself, "When I allow my heart to be fully alive, when I let myself want what my hearts longs for, it hurts too much. Therefore, I will eliminate the part of me that longs most passionately. I will numb the deepest parts of my person. When those parts are put to sleep, when I stop wanting, I hurt so much less." We learn very early how to lessen our pain. We learn that if we allow ourselves to want very little, we are rarely disappointed.

The tragedy of this first step is that the passionate, alive heart that God intended us to offer to others for their joy and well-being is slowly turned off. After a time, we are hardly aware of having a heart to give to others. We become less and less aware of our own desires. Therefore, we are less able to touch those realities in the lives of those around us. Relationships become functional. We no longer enjoy being "passionately there" for others, an experience that was meant to give us joy and confirm our value in God's eyes.

4. a. What do you think of the idea that you've deadened your longing heart?

    b. Are you aware of having done this? What evidence do you see in your life for or against this possibility? (For instance, where do you find yourself indifferent to life, rather than passionately involved?)

LEADER: Read this section aloud, while the group members mark statements they identify with.

A BAD SELF-IMAGE IS BORN

It's hard to imagine the relief a person feels when she deadens her longings. It's comparable, perhaps, to what it feels like to breathe again after having had one's head held under the water to the point of passing out. But the strength of our longing hearts makes it difficult to eliminate the conscious awareness of wanting. Yet when we want, we hurt. This creates a dilemma.

At this point, we go one step further in our effort to make life work without depending on God: *We begin despising those parts of our person that are most passionate and thirsty.* "If I hurt when I want, then my wanting heart must be the problem!"

Therefore, by despising the parts of us that create our dilemma (our loneliness, our deep longings, our desire to share ourselves with others, etc.) we can even more easily justify eliminating those aspects of our person. At a deep level we say, "There is something wrong with me, with who I am as a person. That's why I'm not loved." We take those parts of us that make us most human and call them bad. In so doing, we justify keeping them numb. A picture of the whole process might look like this:

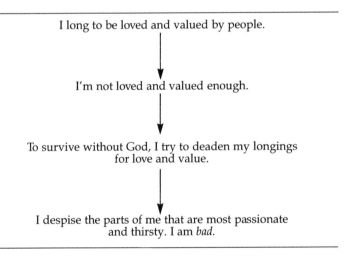

I long to be loved and valued by people.

I'm not loved and valued enough.

To survive without God, I try to deaden my longings for love and value.

I despise the parts of me that are most passionate and thirsty. I am *bad*.

Not wanting has become one of independent humanity's main means of survival in this sinful world. And hating our hungry heart aids us in not wanting. The sad reality is that such efforts do succeed in creating a certain equilibrium; we do survive. But at what a cost! The more we succeed in making this solution work, the more we deaden our hearts to the touch of God, who alone can provide us with the kind of relationship we are so desperately searching for. It's a wonder that when Jesus stood in the midst of a large crowd and cried out, "If anyone is thirsty, let him come to me and drink" (John 7:37), He wasn't overrun with people wanting to take Him up on His offer. We hate being thirsty.

God desires for us as His people to be willing to reawaken our longing hearts, to bring them back to life so that we will move into the lives of people around us. Our aliveness will stir others' hearts out of their numbness in the hope that they, too, will discover their need for living water. But to choose to move in directions that will awaken our hearts puts us back in touch with the painful truths we've learned so well to avoid. In the next session we'll look at why we are generally much more comfortable holding on to our poor self-image, not liking ourselves, than we are with having hearts that are alive.

5. a. What kinds of situations do you avoid because they might expose something about you that you don't like and don't want others to see? (For example, group activities, sports, intellectual endeavors, close relational encounters, being in the public eye, conflicts, and so on.)

   b. What is it about you that you're afraid people will discover?

   c. Why would that be so terrible?

6. At the end of this first session, how are you feeling? (Excited? Frustrated? Hurt? Numb?)

7. What questions do you have about self-image that you're hoping future sessions will answer?

LEADER: Write down the group's questions about self-image. These can help you decide what to focus on in your discussions. You can return to them at the end of your study to see what progress you've made.

STILLNESS

Many groups like to end their meetings with prayer. If your group isn't used to praying aloud together, you could try a simple format. After a few moments of silence, each of you can pray a sentence or two about one of these ideas:

- One thing for which you are *thankful*.

- One thing you would like God to do in your life during this study.

- One thing you would like God to make clearer.

DURING THE WEEK

Make a list of aspects of you that you believe you simply must keep hidden from others if you are to be accepted—parts of you that others can't handle. (These might be emotions, desires, disappointments, sins, enthusiasm, passion. . . .) Bring your list to your next meeting. Don't be afraid to make a complete list—you won't have to read it aloud.

A USEFUL TOOL:
How Not Liking Myself Works for Me

ॐ

1. How did it feel to make a list of the things about
   you that you hide? What did you learn from doing
   that?

> LEADER: While the following material is read
> aloud, the group members should see if they can
> think of their own parallel to the car story.

There is a way that seems right to a man.
(Proverbs 16:25)

THE WAY THAT SEEMS RIGHT

Have you ever noticed what a good motivator guilt is?
I've often wondered how much Christian service and
activity would remain if the guilt that often fuels it were
eliminated. How many people would sit in our pews
on Sunday—in fact, how many church programs would
continue to function—if guilt, as a motivating factor,
were no longer available?

In session 1 we saw that, in spite of our desperate need, we do not seek God, and that this affects the kind of image we begin to form of ourselves. We learn to reduce the pain that comes from wanting what other people aren't offering by calling our longing, thirsty, passionate heart "the problem." We begin to hate the fact that we want what others could provide because wanting it only makes its absence that much more painful. As a result, we develop what I want to call "functional guilt" — guilt over "who we are" as persons. (This is very different from true moral guilt, which is a result of our refusal to listen to God and go His way.)

Now this guilt we feel because of who we are is not simply the result of countless negative messages we receive from our world over the years. Rather, it is an essential tool in sinful man's efforts to make life work without God.

WHEN GIVING WHO YOU ARE BLOWS UP IN YOUR FACE

How does a poor self-image work for me? When I was around ten years old, my father purchased a 1929 Model A Ford with the idea of restoring it to its original condition. He rented the garage across the street from our house, where he spent evenings and weekends working on his project. I remember sitting for hours watching Dad work, handing him tools when he needed them, and feeling a happy sense of being with my father as a part of something important. As the months went by, the whole family could feel the excitement build as each new step was completed and the finished product began to take shape.

Finally, one evening, the end was in sight. Dad drove his trophy into the garage, having just picked it up from the paint shop. The new, black paint glistened in contrast with the yellow spoke wheels and the hand-painted, thin, yellow stripe that outlined the car's silhouette. All that remained to do was screw on the white cloth roof.

To allow his only son to play a more central role in the grand finale, Dad asked me to hold the screwdriver in the slot of the screw while he got inside and turned the nut with a wrench. Once the roof was attached to both sides, the project would be finished at last and we'd be free to walk around and "ooh and ah" over the new family masterpiece. "Be careful," Dad added. "I don't want you to scratch the paint."

I carefully held the screwdriver in the slot of the screw with both hands, while Dad began to turn the wrench from inside the car. All of a sudden, the screwdriver slipped and gouged out a two-inch "ravine" in the black paint on the door of the car. (I can still see the exact shape of that scratch as I write this sentence!) I instantly felt sick to my stomach. Dad jumped out of the car and, upon seeing the scratch, began yelling, screaming, and throwing tools. I remember being very glad my mother was there to come to my rescue.

CONTROL: SOMETHING *I* CAN DO

This was one of those traumatic moments in life when personal survival becomes a priority. I was shaken to the core. I had moved into my world and made who I was available, wanting to have a positive impact. The message had come back: "You bumbling idiot, look at the damage you've done! You can't do anything right!"

For a person who *needs* to know that who they are is valued and desirable, such a message feels like personal death, something akin to free-falling headlong toward the ground. Since I was looking toward those people in my world (and not God) to supply my needs by confirming my value, I was faced with a crisis of unbearable magnitude. I simply had to find a solution—something I could do to increase the chances of never having to feel so worthless again.

Control becomes critical to fallen man's survival. What if I had done what no child ever does and interpreted the event like this? "I'm only human; anyone can make a mistake. Therefore, I'm not a bad person because I scratched the car. The problem is not *me*, but my father's response to my mistake." That sounds like a fair evaluation. But, if that were true, then I as a young boy faced a severe dilemma. I had to avoid such pain at all costs, but if Dad's response were the problem, then for me to avoid further suffering, Dad would have to realize his error and change. I had no control over Dad, and so I would have been helpless to do anything to avoid facing the same kind of pain again. (Independent man hates helplessness.)

But if I could define the problem that caused the painful exchange as *me* — my bumbling, my ineptitude — *then*, as the guilty person, there was something *I* could do to minimize the chances of ever again being told, "You can't do anything right!" This evaluation had little to do with my true ability. It had a lot to do with the goal I needed to accomplish, because if I think *I* am the problem, then there is something *I* can do to provide a solution. Seeing myself as a bumbler became a sort of chart, enabling me to navigate through life avoiding the kinds of situations where I might face rejection — a map that helped me avoid the potential mines of life.

If we think the problem is "the way we are," then we think we can do something about it: We can work hard at learning to do it right next time, or we can move through life avoiding all those situations where "bumblers," for instance, shouldn't go. It's as if we say to ourselves, "I know how to never hurt again, I'll never touch another screwdriver. I'll never go near situations where people are counting on me for something, because I'll only let them down." Feeling guilty about "me" has now become a valuable tool to help me survive in life. Not liking myself gives *me* something *I* can do to minimize pain. And even though not liking who we are is in itself painful, it's a price we're willing to pay to survive.

Had you watched me grow and move through life in the years following that event (and others like it), you would have seen me steering clear of situations where I might have been exposed as inadequate. I avoided things like sports, speaking in front of groups, and close relationships where people might count on and expect something from me. Armed with my negative image, you would have seen me develop a *relational style*, a way of relating to others, that allowed me to avoid the danger of rejection while maximizing the chance of my being desired and valued.

2. What things about you would you most like to change, and how? (Name as many things as you like.)

   ❏ My nose—I'd like it to be smaller.

   ❏ My brain—I'd like to be smarter.

   ❏ My shyness—I'd like to be a brilliant conversationalist.

   Things you would like to change:

3. How do you think your life would be better if these things about you were different?

4. What aspects of your life would you really like to be different?

   ❏ I'd like to be married.

   ❏ I'd like my spouse to love me more.

   ❏ I'd like to make more money.

   Things you wish were different:

5. Do you tend to believe these aspects of life would be different if you were different? Or do you tend more to blame them on someone else? Or do you think, "That's just the way life is"? Explain.

6. Feeling guilty about some aspect of yourself can give you something you can work on to be more likable. How do you go about feeling guilty and working on yourself? What kinds of things do you do?

7. a. Do you feel comfortable sharing some of the items on your list of secrets? Why, or why not?

   b. Share those you feel comfortable revealing.

8. Think of a situation in your life similar to the car-scratching story. Because of that incident, how would you complete this sentence?

   I know how to never hurt again. I'll never. . . .

9. Look at your list from last week. What are you accomplishing by hiding the negative things about yourself (that is, how does not liking these things "work for you")? In what ways do these efforts help you feel more in control of your life?

STILLNESS

As you close in prayer, each participant should have a chance to tell God, "Lord, one thing in my life that I'd really like to have control over is _____."

LEADER: You can end the time of prayer by asking God to help each of you become willing to transfer that control to Him.

DURING THE WEEK

Ask three honest people who know you well to give you five words or phrases that describe you. Bring the list with you to your next meeting.

A RELATIONAL STYLE:
The Result of a Bad Self-Image

᠅

1. a. Take out your list of words with which friends described you this past week. Read one word aloud to the group. How do you feel about that description? (Touched? Hurt? Angry? Grateful? Confused?)

   b. Are you surprised by your friends' descriptions of you? How do they differ from the way you see yourself?

LEADER: As the following section is read aloud, the participants should keep their list of words in mind.

A QUICK REVIEW

We've looked at the adjustments a child makes when she faces the brutal fact that she isn't loved and valued by the people she looks to to meet these essential needs.

By numbing her passionate, desirous heart and wanting less, she reduces the pain she feels. Seeing herself as the cause of her difficulties gives her the hope of coming up with a solution to her life-threatening predicament, a solution she can control.

One important result of this process is that deep inside, the child ends up not liking who she is as a person. A bad self-image has been born! In this session we'll look at how a bad self-image helps determine the kind of person she'll become in the years that follow.

RULES TO LIVE BY

It's true that by hating our passionate heart and seeing ourselves as the problem we are better equipped to protect ourselves from a disappointing world (in logical but very ungodly ways). But the battle is not yet over. We soon discover that, in spite of all those adjustments, we are "stuck" still needing desperately to know we are loved. The longing, thirsty heart God gave us is not easily denied.

All of this leaves us feeling pressure to hide who we really are and yet still wanting to be someone people will like and value. It's as if we say to ourselves, "Now that I've numbed the deepest parts of my person and justified doing so by calling those parts bad, I must still find a way to create a sense of feeling alive."

As a result we begin looking for something we can do to gain some sense of being alive, of being accepted, of mattering, while at the same time avoiding giving who we really are in ways that might bring further rejection. We begin looking for a set of rules by which we can live, a way of acting (or not acting), things we can do (or avoid doing), which will make us more desirable and, therefore, increase our chances of being accepted.

THE MAKING OF A NEW ME

How do we decide which rules to follow in order to become people others might like better? Basically we look at our environment, at the people closest to us, and at our own talents and skills, and ask, "In view of those realities, what can I do that will make me more desirable and grant me a place in my world?"

The boy in session 1 who faced his parents' anger when he asked for a bicycle might have said, "I should be good and not ask for anything. Instead I'll read the desires of the people around me and work hard to respond to them. Then I'll no longer face angry words and mean looks. In fact, people will seem happy with me." He became a man who can never say "no" to another's request, while never asking for a thing for himself. And his relational style works for him. You can imagine how he is liked in his church for his faithful service. The rule he follows is, "Meet the needs of those around you; keep them happy at any cost." When he does, he gets some water for his thirsty soul.

One woman I know recalled that the only time she ever saw her father thrill over her was when she was competent and successful. Today she is an efficient, rather tight woman who masters any challenge she faces with awe-inspiring effectiveness. Few people are drawn to anything resembling relational warmth in her. She hardly seems to notice, as long as she succeeds in bringing the details of her life under control. Her rule, "Be competent," is giving her the impression life is working quite well.

The rule I learned to follow went something like this: "Act in a way that keeps anyone from expecting anything from you. Don't let yourself be taken too seriously or people will count on you and your inadequacy will be exposed. Avoid screwdrivers at all cost!" As a result I became a likable, pleasant guy who kept people at arm's length. I never offered a substantial part of me for others to enjoy — something like a well-frosted but hollow cake.

When I did end up in situations where I had responsibilities, I would spend hours over-preparing, avoiding failure at all cost. When I worked as a part-time teacher in a local high school I arrived daily at

7:30 a.m. and was often seen leaving the school at 10:00 in the evening. No one was going to find me scratching anything! Needless to say, the school board thought I was wonderful. They didn't see a desperate man running frantically to preserve his life.

We've all found rules to live by that work for us. Those rules create a style of relating to others that we live out daily. Some of us have learned to hide behind our good minds. Others are distant and unreachable, never letting anyone see what is happening inside. Still others are compulsive helpers. Many see themselves as black sheep and manage to get rejected constantly; in their minds, rejection confirms they weren't made for close relationships.

2. What aspects of you (your personality, body, mind) were favorably received when you were young? (Which ones got you attention, made others happy, and so on?)

3. As you learned which traits got you something you wanted, what are some of the rules you learned to live by that made you feel more likable and better in control of life?

4. What are some of your other rules?

    ❑ Be competent.

    ❑ Act in a way that keeps anyone from expecting anything from you.

    ❑ Don't let people count on you or your inadequacy will be exposed.

    ❑ Never say no.

    ❑ Never ask for anything.

    ❑ Use your brain.

❑ Silence your emotions.

❑ Don't let anyone see what's inside you.

❑ Get people to reject you so you won't be surprised when they do.

❑ Be in charge.

❑ Never be in charge.

❑ Be a little girl/boy, not an adult.

❑ Be known for your sense of humor.

Your rules:

5. Now connect the list from your friends with your knowledge of yourself. Can you define your relational style in a sentence or two? Get help from the group if you want.

> LEADER: The group could easily spend an entire session on these first five questions. This would be an appropriate place to stop if you have time for an extra session. Each person should write down his or her relational style and try to be aware of using that style this week.
> Ask participants to see if they can identify with any of the effects of a relational style as you read the next section aloud.

HOW OUR RELATIONAL STYLE AFFECTS US

Whatever rules we choose to live by eventually become our god. Our final hope to get what we need to survive is in them. For this reason, our rules also become taskmasters who drive and control us. If being competent brings me "life," then I am condemned to always

having to perform well, to always being "successful."
If being nice to others and meeting their needs is how
I find life, then I can never go "off duty," I can never
relax. The rules we choose to live by become like a
bulky life jacket that keeps us from drowning in the sea
of life, but with time, it grows heavy and uncomfortable. Yet we learn to tolerate the discomfort because it
beats drowning!

HOW OUR RELATIONAL STYLE
AFFECTS OTHERS

When we manage to live according to our rules and
as a result people like us, it tastes so good, it feels like
life itself! In those moments we feel we have a great
self-image. We like the "new me." The tragedy is that
we become so consumed with our efforts to make life
work that we don't even notice, let alone care about,
the impact our relational style is having on the people
around us. We've become totally self-centered.

The rules we follow place tremendous pressure on
the people around us. If my survival depends on never
being exposed as inadequate, woe to you if you bring to
light a failure in my life. And you'll sense the require-
ment to accept me as I am and never point out where
I'm wrong. If "meeting others' needs" is the rule I follow, you'll sense the pressure to let me know how much
you appreciate me. The relational style that results from
our rule-keeping creates a "pull" on others to come
through for us, to cooperate so our rules will have the
result they were intended to have. If you respond the
way I need you to, I'll probably like you. If you don't,
watch out! In the end, people won't feel loved by me,
but manipulated and used, which is in fact exactly how
they ought to feel.

Self-centeredness has now been perfected. Fueled
by a negative self-image, we have found ways to relate
with others that win us some sense of being liked. And
by these sinful methods we're left with the impression
that life actually works pretty well without God. How

can this process be undone? How does change that deals with these realities take place? In the next session we'll look at how we can move toward becoming other-centered people, free to make our hearts available to others in ways that encourage and give a taste of life and grace.

6. Look again at the ways your friends described you. How would you say these people feel "pulled" to come through for you, to cooperate so your rules will have the result you intended them to have? (For example, "They know they have to be grateful." "She knows she has to keep showing she's impressed with my competence." "When I act helpless, they know I expect them to feel sorry for me, pay attention to me, and help me accomplish the task.")

7. a. Christian legalism is rooted in keeping rules in order to achieve approval (from God or people). What "Christian" rules have you followed in order to be approved by people?

   b. What things do you feel you must keep doing in order for the Lord to be pleased with you?

God described Israel's worship of idols like this:

"My people have committed two sins:
They have forsaken me,
    the spring of living water,
and have dug their own cisterns,
    broken cisterns that cannot hold water."
        (Jeremiah 2:13)

8. a. How is keeping rules like digging one's own cistern?

   b. Can you identify with the image of working hard to keep a leaky cistern full of water? What's that like for you?

9. *(Optional)* Think of a time recently when you've had one of the following reactions to some person or event:

   ❑ Anger

   ❑ Anxiety

   ❑ Pulling away

   ❑ Trying harder

   ❑ Smoothing things over

   ❑ Demanding your own way

   ❑ Losing yourself in busyness

   ❑ Pushing others to cooperate and accept you

   How does your reaction reveal the requirements you're placing on that person or situation?

10. *(Optional)* Consider the man who was a compulsive helper. What's the difference between this man's "Christian service" and actions that are truly centered on loving others?

11. a. How are you feeling about yourself right now?

   b. What would you normally tend to do with
      those feelings? (Forget about them? Enjoy them?
      Laugh them away? Have an argument with your
      spouse? Drink a chocolate milkshake? Get by
      yourself and cry? Talk with God about them?)

STILLNESS

Pray in small groups — pairs or threes — about the things
you each do to keep your leaky cisterns full of water.
You can just tell God what you do and ask for the grace
to abandon your self-made cisterns.

DURING THE WEEK

Watch for a time this week when you are using your
relational style and it is working for you. (People are
approving, paying attention, not asking too much, toe-
ing the line, or whatever.) As soon as possible after you
notice this, jot down a quick note to remind yourself:
"My relational style of _____ is working to
get people to _____."

THE PATH TO CHANGE

ॐ

1. How would you describe your relational style during the past three hours? Have you been using the typical one you identified in session 3?

LEADER: Read the following aloud.

WHAT NEEDS TO CHANGE?

We've seen how we get a poor self-image and why we cling to it even when it hurts us. But how can we break free from that way of life?

It's easy to fall into thinking, *I don't like myself because the people in my world have not treated me as a valuable, lovable person. If they had treated me with love and respect, I would have learned to like myself better.* The assumption is that my environment, by interacting with me in certain ways, has caused my negative view of myself. Therefore, getting my environment to treat me better becomes the key to having a good self-image.

Had my father reacted graciously when I scratched his Model A Ford, I might not have come away feeling

43

I was a "bad person" because I made a mistake. But then, couldn't each of us point to thousands of events in our lives where, had the people involved reacted differently, our self-image would not have been damaged? *If my good self-image depends on others treating me as a valuable person, then I'm condemned to either (1) keep trying to get better responses from the people around me, or (2) learn to better insulate myself against the negative effects of their disapproval.* I need either better performance or higher walls.

Efforts to change self-image by providing positive feedback to offset the negative messages of the past do not get down to the true, deep-seated problem. They only reinforce the very rule-keeping that hides both the bad self-image and the inner dynamics that sustain it. Such an approach simply leaves us feeling a little more justified in being angry (or devastated) when the people in our world don't come through for us. Often we encourage people to like themselves better without facing or dealing with their core refusal to depend on God for life. If we do this, we've only helped sinners function more effectively without God. This is the very essence of humanism. How, then, does self-image change?

2. Why do you think people are attracted to the idea that their bad self-image is caused by hurts they've suffered?

3. If the only way to get a good self-image were to be applauded by others, where would that leave you? How would you feel and what would you do?

THE DILEMMA

Imagine floating in the ocean, your head kept above
the water by an inner tube around you. The inner tube
is bulky, tight, and rubs you under your arms. It also
has a slow leak, requiring that you regularly pump
air into it in order not to sink. But as long as you keep
pumping, it keeps you afloat, and for that you're
thankful.

Surrounding you in the water are dozens of people.
Many, like yourself, are managing to survive by using
their energy to pump air into their inner tubes at regu-
lar intervals. These folks seem cheerful and are even
willing to carry on short conversations in between
pumping sessions. But a large number of the people
around you are thrashing in the water in great panic.
They have lost the energy or motivation to keep pumping and their inner tubes have become flaccid. Ter-
ror shows in their eyes as the water laps up around
their mouths and noses. Several are on the verge of
drowning, crying out desperately for help. The water is
strewn with unmanned inner tubes, floating like flat-
tened doughnuts.

Your dilemma is obvious. If you try to help the
ill-fated people around you, you won't be able to give
the necessary attention to your own inner tube. To keep
from drowning, you must ignore the plight of those
around you.

This is the self-image dilemma. If "keeping rules"
gives us a sense of life, of being loved and valued, then
choosing to not keep those rules means death. Therefore, the relational style we've developed that grants us

"life" consumes all our energy and takes priority over the needs of others. As long as our selfish strategies work, we function quite well and can even "relate" to others who are also managing to make life work. But our system requires all our energy. The needs and struggles of others (to the degree they don't fit into our rule-keeping) only remind us of our own vulnerability and make us "pump" all the harder.

THE BASIS FOR CHANGE

Then one day as you're floating along giving your inner tube the occasional squeeze to see if it needs air, you hear the voice of God. He says that you matter to Him, so much that He's engraved you on the palms of His hands (Isaiah 49:16), that He's committed to you, and that He will never let you drown. He adds that He is most honored and pleased when you demonstrate His love for you by loving the people around you.

At this point, you're confronted with a choice. You can turn your back on God and keep pouring all your energy into maintaining your inner tube. Or you can choose to take God at His word and throw your pump into the next wave that comes your way. The first choice would leave things in *your* hands with something *you* can keep doing to guarantee your safety. The second, as demonstrated by your swimming up to the closest struggling person, would bear witness to the reliability, the trustworthiness of God.

Of course the dilemma centers on the question, "Will I really survive if I abandon my support system and use my energies to love others?" Perhaps in more biblical terms the question would be, "Is it true that if I lose my life I will find it, and that if I hold on to my life I will lose it?" (See Matthew 10:39.) We tend to wait for the assurance that we will survive before giving up those things that work to provide us with "life." But we'll never experience the liberation of God's care until we act on what He declares by relinquishing the source of life—what we use to replace Him. The only

way to know if we'll *really* survive is to abandon our
inner tubes, to give up the systems we use to make life
work for us.

CHANGE IN ACTION

What does it look like practically when a person
chooses to trust God and give up his or her source of
life? The answer is as broad as the number of relational
styles the human race has devised to make life work
without God.

The controlled, competent woman from session 3
would begin turning her energy toward others, making
her heart available in warm, tender ways to encourage
and comfort the people around her. Giving up her inner
tube might mean spontaneously inviting people over in
spite of a dirty house. It might be seen in her choice to
read a book to her child for an hour before bed, rather
than go over tomorrow's Bible study "just one more
time." She would begin opening her heart to others, letting them see real needs they could touch.

Repentance for the man who became a compulsive
helper would be to honestly share his heart because
of another's need instead of working to guarantee his
acceptance. He would wisely choose not to say yes
to every request and opportunity for service, risking
disappointing others. You would see him expressing
opinions that might not be popular (he may have to
develop some first!). He might ask his wife to bring him
a soda from the kitchen instead of always being the
one who gets things for others. He would stop hiding
behind his service and would begin giving others an
opportunity to reach out to him by making his needs
known.

As varied as the expressions of repentance might
be, the result will always be the same: other-centered
love. The person God made you to be will no longer be
despised and hidden away but freed to bless others as
a testimony of His liberating care and love. Repenting
of our selfishness liberates us to join God in His eternal

project of setting people free—something slaves cannot do. As Jesus told us, "By this all men will know that you are my disciples, if you love one another" (John 13:35).

The path to deep change is not easy. The only way to change quickly is to settle for surface change and just start living by a different set of rules. Deep change requires us to face the anguish of our souls that set the whole process of hating and hiding who we are in motion in the first place. In the final session we will talk about the motivation that is necessary if we are going to walk "the unlikely path that leads to life."

4. Since the last session, you've been alert for a time when your relational style was succeeding in maintaining your self-image. Now think of the people you encountered during that time (your spouse or roommate, your kids, your friends, your colleagues). How do you think you affected them? How were they probably inclined to feel about themselves and about you?

5. a. God promises to care for your life (keep you from drowning). What feelings does this stir up in you?

   b. Why do you suppose you feel that way?

6. a. What would honoring Him by throwing away your pump (your attempts to keep your life afloat) look like practically?

b. Who are the people around you who would ben-
efit most from this change in your life, and how
would they be affected?

We can expect some negative reactions when we
stop doing the things we did to win approval. When
the compulsive helper starts saying no, he may well
encounter anger.

7. *(Optional)* What are some of the negative reactions
you might expect from people if you change?

When we stop keeping our familiar rules, we are confronted anew with the deep personal realities that
started the self-image process in motion in the first
place. We may stop feeling accepted, important, and in
control of our survival.

8. *(Optional)* How does that prospect make you feel?

9. What is your biggest fear tied to giving up your
rule-keeping?

STILLNESS

As you close in prayer, tell God how you feel about
throwing away your pump (your rules). You can divide
into groups of two or three for this if you want. Genu-
inely throwing away our pumps is impossible without
God. Pray for your partner(s) about this.

49

DURING THE WEEK

Think about throwing your self-preservation supports and rules away and, instead, relying on God for personal survival. See if you can identify what doing this would look like in one specific situation you are currently facing.

THE PROCESS OF CHANGE

෧

1. Did you think about throwing away your survival rules this week? What opportunities for doing this did you notice, and how did you seize them?

> LEADER: Read the following aloud together.

CHANGE THAT GOES DEEP

Genuine, deep, heart-level change is complex. I sometimes envy people who hold a "Name it and claim it" or a "Do what's right and everything else will fall into place" approach to Christian growth. Our discussion of self-image seems so complicated in comparison! The problem is, biblical change is neither superficial nor simple. We want to be transformed into the likeness of Christ with ever-increasing glory (2 Corinthians 3:18). This process involves a renewal of our person at the level of the hidden thoughts and motivations of our hearts. It requires that we "renew our minds" (Romans 12:1-2), which certainly includes the dynamics we've been discussing.

While I don't like it sometimes, I believe God's sanctifying work requires us to face realities that humble and undo us and that push us finally to concur passionately, "Only God is sufficient for these things!" It seems we only discover God when we come to the end of ourselves. Being humbled is a prerequisite for being lifted up. (See James 4:10, 1 Peter 5:5-6.)

Why, then, walk this path? Why not simply adopt an approach to the Christian life that allows us to make some external adjustments and avoid being shaken to the core by the exposure of the hidden purposes of our hearts? If my relational style works reasonably well, why mess things up by facing the commitment to self-sufficiency that undergirds it?

2. What's your gut-level reaction to an approach to the Christian life that promises to humble and undo you and push you to discover that "only God is sufficient for these things"?

❏ I can't wait. I love pain.

❏ I like stability, so this scares me.

❏ I see now that my rules are getting me what I want, so why should I change?

❏ I'm scared, but I'm willing to move at least a little, because I realize that something is desperately wrong.

❏ I'm miserable now, so what do I have to lose?

❏ The whole idea of unsettling everything makes me angry!

Your reaction:

LEADER: While the next section is read, each
person should consider whether he or she has this
kind of hunger for change.

A HUNGER FOR CHANGE

I'm more and more convinced a person will not change
significantly if he can't proclaim with a certain amount
of conviction and passion, "I really *want* to go God's
way." Not, "I really *ought* to go God's way," but rather,
"The bottom line in my heart is I deeply *want* God's
way." How does a person come to such a point? Two
elements are involved.

The first element is linked to what happens inside
me when I see how my self-centered relational style
affects the people around me. When I realize I'm floating along pumping my inner tube while letting my
spouse, my child, or a friend drown, something deep
within me reacts. I don't want to treat others that way!
When I recognize how my self-protective strategies say,
"Life works better without You, God!" I am profoundly
shaken. I don't want to thumb my nose at God!

Suddenly, I'm gripped in my "heart of flesh and
not of stone" (Ezekiel 36:26) by the ugliness of my sin
as reflected in my relationships with others. I face the
contradiction in my life and concur deep within that
the way I'm living is wrong and deserves judgment.
Functional guilt, guilt over "who I am" that pushes me
to work harder to be better, gives way to true guilt, and
I'm stopped in my tracks. This is the first step toward
developing a hunger for change.

Second, gripped by the gravity of my sin, I turn
to the Lord expecting an angry look and harsh words.
Instead, I meet this unique Person who, without min-
imizing my sin, opens His arms to embrace me. I hear
Him declare, "Yes, it's ugly, that's why I had to die.
Because of My death, an intimate relationship between
you and Me is possible, right now." I encounter God's

grace on my behalf—a relationship of unwavering love, when I *deserve* judgment.

3. Are you aware of having a hunger to repent? If you are, how did you get to that point? If not, what do you suppose stands in the way?

4. How do you tend to react when you get "caught with your pants down," when you are confronted undeniably with your selfishness?

5. What means do you tend to use to avoid being caught and humbled by your sin? (Trying harder to be good to make up for it? Arguing your way out of it? Shifting blame? Retreating?)

THE PATH TO REPENTANCE

How do these two elements—sorrow over my sin and God's gracious response—work together to produce a hunger in my heart for change? When I see how much damage my efforts to make life work have caused, I'm confronted with the utter failure of my decision to function without God. I get an "up close and personal" view of Proverbs 14:12—"There is a way that seems right to a man, but in the end it leads to death." Facing my selfishness exposes my desperately deceitful heart for which I have no solution (Jeremiah 17:9). It also robs me of the illusion of being able to fix things on my own. It "humbles me" so that being "lifted up" by God becomes a desperate necessity.

That's when the second element, the Lord's grace, exposes the foolishness of my sinful direction even more.

I discover the love and importance I've been working so hard to earn is already fully provided in my relationship with Him. I realize His love and acceptance have nothing to do with my being lovable, for here He is loving me at my worst. His warm embrace robs me of the useful tool of calling "who I am" the problem. God's grace beckons me to give up my independence to come and drink what He offers. In contrast with this "spring of living water," my "broken cisterns" look pretty absurd (Jeremiah 2:13)!

What takes place in my heart when I face these realities? In 2 Corinthians 7:9 Paul states, "Your sorrow led you to repentance." In Romans 2:4 he says that God's "kindness leads you toward repentance." Facing my sin and God's grace creates a *hunger in my heart* to change, a deep desire to repent, to abandon my self-centered strategies and to go God's way. Rule-keeping gives way to the freedom to love others.

6. In which relationship are you gripped by the ugliness of your sin, by the ways your relational style has hurt that person?

7. a. How do you react to the image of being warmly embraced by a loving God when you least deserve it?

   b. What, if anything, keeps you from discovering the Lord in this way?

LEADER: While these words are read aloud, group members should try to be aware of the feelings stirred up inside them.

THE FRUIT OF REPENTANCE

"Repentance" as it relates to self-image is a choice to trust God with what is most vital to us, our own soul. Leaping into the turbulent waters of life to help others is stupid if there is no one there to care for our soul and keep us from drowning. On the other hand, if God is there like He says He is, missing the opportunity to be a coworker with Him by loving others is stupid. What results when a person chooses to take God at His word and make his or her heart available to others with their well-being in mind? What is the fruit of repentance?

Our Image of God Begins to Change

Many of us view God as distant, a little uptight, and not really that interested in us. Our independent strategies for making life work only reinforce such an image: We work hard to make it on our own as if we had an absent father. Giving up those strategies leaves room for God's faithful care to be demonstrated. We "taste" that the Lord is good, not because people suddenly begin cooperating and loving us the way we'd like, but because, in the face of rejection, we really don't "drown." The image of a loving, involved Father becomes increasingly real.

"Because you are my help, I sing in the shadow of your wings. My soul clings to you; your right hand upholds me" (Psalm 63:7-8). Like David the psalmist, when we entrust our personal survival to the Lord we discover a growing ability to testify with deep conviction to our heavenly Father's life-sustaining presence.

Our Image of Ourselves Begins to Change

As we give up living as "failures" who must hide who we are or work hard to change, we begin to get a wondrous taste of being alive on God's behalf. Turning away from our manipulative relational styles and deadness, our redeemed hearts are increasingly instruments of blessing to others. We taste the joy of becoming the persons God intended us to be.

FIGHT THE GOOD FIGHT!
(1 Timothy 6:12)

Late last evening I finished writing this final session. I have to admit to basking somewhat in the glory of having completed what had, at times, seemed like a formidable task. I'd faced my fears and managed to put my thoughts on paper in a reasonably logical sequence, and I was enjoying the moment. My experience even seemed to confirm all I'd said so far.

Then this morning when my alarm went off it happened once more. I was overcome all over again with the same sense of inadequacy I described in the introduction of this guide. So let me add this final point. Becoming the other-centered men and women God designed us to be doesn't happen quickly or easily. It's a battle. But if we choose not to flee, the battle becomes the context where we not only grow into people who glorify and honor God more and more, but we also discover and fall in love with the Lord Himself. And for that reason alone, it is a "good" fight.

8. What feelings are stirred in you when you think about being gripped by God's love and becoming a coworker with God by loving others?

Fruit, like an apple or an orange, is the end result of a process that is crucial and often hidden. The "fruits of repentance" are not things we should necessarily try to understand or even make happen. But as we actively trust God with our souls by giving up our broken cisterns, these fruits will begin to take form and we should be able to recognize and enjoy them, giving God the glory for their presence in our lives.

9. What path do you see ahead of you that gives you hope of tasting the fruits mentioned above?

STILLNESS

In closing, each person should have a chance to tell God how he or she is feeling. Take the opportunity to thank Him for what you've learned, to ask Him questions only He can answer, and to ask Him for the courage and persistence to pursue change.

HELP FOR LEADERS

Ȥa

This guide is designed to be discussed in a group of from four to twelve people. Because God has designed Christians to function as a body, we learn and grow more when we interact with others than we would on our own. If you are on your own, see if you can recruit a few other people to join you in working through this guide. You can use the guide on your own, but you'll probably long for someone to talk with about it. On the other hand, if you have a group larger than twelve we suggest that you divide into smaller groups of six or so for discussion. With more than twelve people, you begin to move into a large group dynamic, and not everyone has the opportunity to participate.

The following pages are designed to help a discussion leader guide the group in an edifying time centered on God's truth and grace. You may want one appointed person to lead all the sessions, or you may want to rotate leadership.

PREPARATION

Your aim as a leader is to create an environment that encourages people to feel safe enough to be honest with themselves, the group, and God. Group members should sense that no question is too dumb to ask, that the other participants will care about them no matter what they reveal about themselves, and that each person's opinion is as valid as everyone else's. At the same time, they should know that the Bible is your final authority for what is true.

As the group leader, your most important preparation for each session is prayer. You will want to make your prayers personal, of course, but here are some suggestions:

- Pray that group members will be able to attend the discussion consistently. Ask God to enable them to feel safe enough to share vulnerable thoughts and feelings honestly, and to contribute their unique gifts and insights.

- Pray for group members' private times with God. Ask Him to be active in nurturing each person.

- Ask the Holy Spirit for guidance in exercising patience, acceptance, sensitivity, and wisdom. Pray for an atmosphere of genuine love in the group, with each member being honestly open to learning and change.

- Pray that your discussion will lead each of you to obey the Lord more closely and demonstrate His presence to others.

- Pray for insight and wisdom as you lead the group.

After prayer, your most important preparation is to be thoroughly familiar with the material you will discuss. Before each meeting, be sure to read the text and answer all of the questions for yourself. This will prepare you to think ahead of questions group members might raise.

Choose a time and place to meet that is consistent, comfortable, and relatively free from distractions.

Refreshments can help people mingle, but don't let this consume your study and discussion time.

LEADING THE GROUP

It should be possible to cover each session in sixty minutes, but you will probably find yourself wishing you had two hours to talk about each group member's situation. As you conduct each session keep the following in mind.

Work toward a safe, relaxed, and open atmosphere. This may not come quickly, so as the leader you must model acceptance, humility, openness to truth and change, and love. Develop a genuine interest in each person's remarks, and expect to learn from them. Show that you care by listening carefully. Be affirming and sincere. Sometimes a hug is the best response—sometimes a warm silence is.

Pay attention to how you ask questions. By your tone of voice, convey your interest in and enthusiasm for the question and your warmth toward the group. The group members will adopt your attitude. Read the questions as though you were asking them of good friends.

If the discussion falters, keep these suggestions in mind:

- Be comfortable with silence. Let the group wrestle to think of answers. Some of the questions require thought or reflection on one's life. Don't be quick to jump in and rescue the group with your answers.

- On the other hand, you should answer questions yourself occasionally. In particular, you should be the first to answer questions about personal experiences. In this way you will model the depth of vulnerability you hope others will show. Count on this: If you are open, others will be too, and vice versa. Don't answer every question, but don't be a silent observer.

61

- Reword a question if you perceive that the group has trouble understanding it as written.

- If a question evokes little response, feel free to leave it and move on.

- When discussion is winding down on a question, go on to the next one. It's not necessary to push people to see every angle.

Ask only one question at a time. Often, participants' responses will suggest a follow-up question to you. Be discerning as to when you are following a fruitful train of thought and when you are going on a tangent.

Be aware of time. It's important to honor the commitment to end at a set time.

Encourage constructive controversy. The group members can learn a great deal from struggling with the many sides of an issue. If you aren't threatened when someone disagrees, the whole group will be more open and vulnerable. Intervene when necessary, making sure that people debate ideas and interpretations, not attack each other's feelings or character. If the group gets stuck in an irreconcilable argument, say something like, "We can agree to disagree here," and move on.

Be someone who facilitates, rather than an expert. People feel more prone to contributing with a peer leader than with a "parent" leader. Allow the group members to express their feelings and experiences candidly.

Encourage autonomy with the group members. With a beginning group, you may have to ask all the questions and do all the planning. But within a few meetings you should start delegating various leadership tasks. Help members learn to exercise their gifts. Let them start making decisions and solving problems together. Encourage them to maturity and unity in Christ.

Validate both feelings and objective facts. Underneath the umbrella of Scripture, there is room for both. Often people's feelings are a road map to a biblical truth. Give them permission for feelings and facts.

Summarize the discussion. Summarizing what has been said will help the group members see where the discussion is going and keep them more focused.

Don't feel compelled to "finish." It would be easy to spend an entire session on one or two questions. As leader, you will be responsible to decide when to cut off one discussion and move to another question, and when to let a discussion go on even though you won't have time for some questions. If there are more questions than you need, you can select those that seem most helpful.

Let the group plan applications. The "During the Week" sections are suggestions. Your group should adapt them to be relevant and life-changing for the members. If people see a genuine need that an application addresses, they are more likely to follow up. Help them see the connection between need and application.

End with refreshments. This gives people an excuse to stay for a few extra minutes and discuss the subject informally. Often the most important conversations occur after the formal session.

DURING THE FIRST SESSION

You or someone else in the group can open the session with a short prayer dedicating your time to God.

It is significant how much more productive and honest a discussion is if the participants know each other. The questions in this session are designed to help participants get acquainted. You can set an example of appropriate disclosure by being the first to answer some questions. Participants will be looking to you to let them know how much honesty is safe in this group. If you reveal your worst secrets in the first session, you may scare some people away. Conversely, if you conceal anything that might make you look bad, participants will get the message that honesty isn't safe.

At some point during the session, go over the following guidelines. They will help make your discussion more fruitful, especially when you're dealing with issues that truly matter to people.

Confidentiality. No one should repeat what someone shares in the group unless that person gives permission. Even then, discretion is imperative. Be trustworthy. Participants should talk about their own feelings and experiences, not those of others.

Attendance. Each session builds on previous ones, and you need continuity with each other. Ask group members to commit to attending all five sessions unless an emergency arises.

Participation. This is a *group* discussion, not a lecture. It is important that each person participates in the group.

Honesty. Appropriate openness is a key to a good group. Be who you really are, not who you think you should be. On the other hand, don't reveal inappropriate details of your life simply for the shock value. The goal is relationship.